I HAD A *Friend* NAMED PETER

Talking to Children
About the Death of a Friend

JANICE COHN, D.S.W.

Illustrated by

GAIL OWENS

William Morrow and Company, Inc. / New York

This book is dedicated to the memory of
Marc Berman,
and to those of his friends—both children
and adults—who shared their feelings about his death with me, in the hope that
it might help others.

The author warmly thanks Dr. Robert Stevenson, who read
each draft of this manuscript and contributed his ideas, insight,
and support; Dr. Sandra Fox, whose example and encourage-
ment were crucial in the creation of the Helping Children in
Crisis program and the subsequent writing of this book; and
lastly, David Reuther, who initiated this project and whose
vision and belief in its value made the book a reality.

Printed in the United States of America.

1 2 3 4 5 6 7 8 9 10

Library of Congress Cataloging-in-Publication Data

Cohn, Janice.
I had a friend named Peter.

Summary: When Betsy learns about the death of a
friend, her parents and teacher answer questions
about dying, funerals, and the burial process.

[1. Death—Fiction] I. Owens, Gail, ill.
II. Title.
PZ7.C665Iac 1987   [E]   86-31150
ISBN 0-688-06685-2   ISBN 0-688-06686-0 (lib. bdg.)

INTRODUCTION

When a young child dies because of an accident or illness, most parents and teachers are faced with a terrible dilemma: Should the child's friends and classmates be told what has happened? Does hiding or altering the truth "protect" children or ultimately harm them? How much information should children be given?

While there is no "right" way to help children who are confronted with the death of a friend, experts in the fields of child development, psychology, and social work do suggest certain guidelines.

When do children usually begin to understand the concept of death?

Whatever economic or cultural background the children may be from, their understanding of death is mainly influenced by their age. In general, children under five years of age usually do not understand that death is final and universal—that all living things eventually die. Children of about six through nine years of age tend to think of death as a person—a shadowy figure that can be thwarted or outsmarted if they only knew how! When children are ten years of age and older, they can usually understand what death means, and ponder such concepts as an afterlife.

Though many young children are not able to grasp fully the concept of death, parents and teachers *can* lay the groundwork for a more complete understanding by being receptive and honest in responding to children's questions about death.

What is the best way to explain death to a young child?

Young children need to be helped to understand that death is a biological process; that when people (or pets) have died, their bodies stop working and they can no longer move or speak, think, or feel anything at all. Do *not* compare death with sleep. This can be potentially disturbing for young children, since they may confuse the two concepts and develop sleep problems.

It should be emphasized that death is "forever"; when someone has died, they can't become alive again. But it takes time for children to grasp this concept fully, as well as to grasp the fact that death is universal. Parents and teachers will probably have to reintroduce these ideas to young children a number of times before they fully understand.

Should children be told about the death of a friend? Won't they be frightened that the same thing might happen to them?

It is important to be honest with children when a friend has died. Children often have an uncanny ability to sense when something sad and upsetting has happened. If no one explains what is going on, children are left to cope alone with their fears and fantasies. Often this is even more upsetting than the truth, particularly if children suspect that their parents and teachers are hiding something from them. An important message to give children is that *nothing* is too sad or terrible to talk about with a parent or other caring adult.

How should young children be told about the death of a friend?

Simply and honestly, tell the child what has happened, then wait to see the kinds of questions the child asks. Take your cues from the child about how much information to give. Many times, children will ask the same questions again and again. This does not necessarily mean your answer has not been a sensitive or helpful one; it's simply part of the process that helps children cope with something that is confusing or frightening.

Initially, some children ask no questions at all and seem to have little interest in talking or thinking about what has happened. Such children may find it very hard to express their feelings in words. When this happens, it is best not to press children to talk before they are ready, but rather to let them know that when they *are* ready, you will be available to talk with them.

It is very important that when children do express their feelings, these are acknowledged and supported, rather than minimized. Do not try to distract children or "cheer them up" by suggesting a trip to the circus or buying them toys. When children are upset, it's more helpful to say "I can see you are worried," or "I know that what we are talking about is very scary," rather than "You'll feel better soon."

Giving children the opportunity to express and share their feelings with the adults they love and depend upon helps them to work through their fears and confusion.

Are children capable of grieving?

Young children are usually capable of mourning and grieving, but it's important to realize that children may show their distress in a number of ways—not necessarily by being sad and tearful. Frequently children "act out" their feelings, rather than talk about them. One child might become boisterous and provocative, while another might be silent and withdrawn. Behavior problems and difficulties in concentrating are not uncommon, nor are nightmares, stomachaches, and headaches.

Sometimes children seem not to care at all. When they are told about the death of a good friend, they seem to show no emotion or they may become silly and giggly. Many times this means that these children are so overwhelmed by anxiety or sadness that their emotions become essentially "frozen" or reversed into giddiness. This will eventually pass.

Some children feel there is something wrong with them if they are unable to cry or feel the kind of sadness that others around them may be showing. That's why it is important to stress that we all have our own special way of showing our feelings, and there is no one "right" way to behave.

Should a child be allowed to go to a friend's funeral?

Mental health experts agree that it can be a good experience for children to go to a funeral, as a way of saying good-bye. However, children should never be pressured into attending if they do not want to go. And if they do attend, they should be prepared for what will happen at the funeral. But keep in mind that many young children do not have the patience to sit still during the entire ceremony, and may need to leave before the end of the service.

Sometimes children will ask to go to the burial service at the cemetery. There is no evidence that this is harmful to children, as long as they are prepared for what will occur.

Whether children attend a funeral and burial service or not, they are often greatly helped by being given the opportunity to say good-bye in some way to the child who died. Children will be comforted to learn that people we have loved and cared about are always kept alive in our memories. Encouraging children to think of ways that they can help themselves and others remember their friend (for example, by drawing a picture or planting a flower) contributes to the healing process by allowing them to commemorate the death.

Should young children be told about heaven, or an afterlife?

Every family has its own beliefs about God, heaven, and an afterlife. It is always appropriate for parents to tell children what they believe, and state that this is their belief. Frequently, this can be a source of comfort for the child. However, while it may be consoling to say that the deceased person is continuing to exist in some other form or place, and that he or she continues to love and care for the child, it is not advisable to tell children that a loved person is up in heaven, looking down upon them. Though it would seem that such an idea would be reassuring, in reality it can be a burden for children to feel that every time they do something naughty or mischievous, the dead person is observing and possibly judging them.

What kind of reactions are "normal" for children after the death of a friend?

Some children may become deeply upset when a friend has died. When this happens, it's especially important for parents and teachers to try to learn the *nature* of the distress. For example, some children become upset because of the loss of their friend, or because they are afraid they, too, might die, or because a friend's death has brought back feelings associated with an earlier death or loss. Other children think that they have caused a death in some way. This is because young children really do believe in magic—they think that their thoughts and wishes can actually cause things to occur. Once you have found out why children are upset, you can better comfort them and address the fears or misconceptions they may have.

After children learn of the death of a friend, they might experience some sleep difficulties, nightmares, or other physical symptoms for a while. They also might show some behavior changes, or regress to some past behaviors, such as bedwetting or thumb sucking. There is nothing abnormal about these reactions. However, if they persist for many weeks, or are so intense that they interfere with a child's regular activities, it would be helpful to seek out a professional consultation.

Children who have experienced a previous death or loss, children who have had previous emotional problems, and children who may have had some responsibility in a death (or think that they have) are at a higher risk of developing problems that require professional help. Parents can obtain information about acquiring a psychiatric evaluation of their child from their community's mental health association, mental health center, or the pediatric psychiatry department of the nearest medical center.

Betsy had a special friend named Peter. They liked to paint and ride their bicycles and play with toys. Sometimes they would get mad at each other, but mostly they had fun doing things together.

One evening, Betsy's parents came into her room and said that they wanted to talk to her about something very sad, and even a little scary. Then her parents took her in their arms and told her that there had been an accident. Her friend Peter had been hit by a car. "Hit by a car," repeated Betsy slowly. "What happened?"

"This afternoon, Peter was playing ball in front of the house," said her father. "When the ball rolled into the street, Peter ran after it and forgot to look for cars. He didn't see a car coming around the bend, and even though the driver tried very hard to stop, there wasn't enough time. Peter was hurt so badly that the doctors couldn't make him better, and he died."

Betsy was confused at first, because she wasn't sure what it meant to die. "Will I see Peter again?" she asked. "No," said her mother. "You won't see Peter again. You see, Betsy, when Peter died, his body stopped working. Now he can't move or speak, or feel anything at all—not the touch of someone's hands, or the wind, or anything that can hurt him."

"But where is Peter *now?*" Betsy asked.

Her mother said, "Right now his body is in a special room in the hospital called a morgue. In a few days, he will be buried in the ground. After a while, his body will become part of the earth, and will help other living things like trees and flowers to grow."

"But if he's in the ground, won't he be cold and lonely? It sounds like it will be so scary for him."

"Yes, it does sound like it would be scary," agreed her mother. "But remember, Betsy, Peter isn't alive, and so he can't feel scared because he can't feel anything at all."

Betsy thought for a moment and asked, "But when will Peter be put in the ground? And who will put him there?"

Her mother said, "Peter will be buried in the ground during a special ceremony called a funeral. His family and many of his friends will be there, to see him be buried. Daddy and I will be there, too."

"Can I come?" asked Betsy excitedly.

"Would you like to?" said her father.

Betsy thought for a moment and said, "I think so, if it isn't too scary."

"Would you like me to tell you what I think will happen at the funeral?" asked her father.

"Oh, yes," said Betsy.

"Well, as I said, there will be lots of people there who loved and cared about Peter. Most people will be feeling very sad, and some of them may be crying. But it's very good when this happens, because when people show their feelings and share them with others, they usually begin to feel better."

"Then what happens?"

"Well, the minister and some other people who knew and loved Peter will talk a little bit about him."

"What will they say?" asked Betsy, very interested.

"They will talk about what he was like, and some of the things that he said and did. They might even remember some funny things which will make people laugh, even though they are feeling sad."

"But when will Peter be put in the ground?" insisted Betsy.

"I was coming to that," said her father. "After everyone has spoken, the people will ride to a place called a cemetery where people are buried in the ground, after they have died. Peter's body will be in a special box called a casket—which is made very soft inside—and the casket will be put in the ground after the minister says a special prayer for Peter."

"And then what?" asked Betsy.

"Then people will gather together at Peter's house to talk about and remember him, and to comfort one another and maybe cry together."

"Do you think you'd like to go to Peter's funeral with Daddy and me?" said Betsy's mother.

Betsy was quiet for a moment. "I don't know. Can I tell you in the morning?"

"That's fine," said her father.

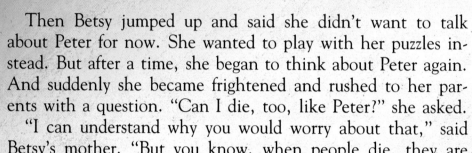

Then Betsy jumped up and said she didn't want to talk about Peter for now. She wanted to play with her puzzles instead. But after a time, she began to think about Peter again. And suddenly she became frightened and rushed to her parents with a question. "Can I die, too, like Peter?" she asked.

"I can understand why you would worry about that," said Betsy's mother. "But you know, when people die, they are usually quite old, and have lived for many years, and they have had the chance to see and do many things. Once in a very great while, a child dies, as Peter did. But almost all little boys and girls grow up, finish school, go to work, and have children of their own."

"Will I do that?" asked Betsy.

"I'm sure you will," answered her mother as she gave her a warm hug.

Betsy felt better after hearing that. But later she had a stomachache, and when she went to sleep that night, she awakened from a dream that had frightened her. She cried out for her parents, who came to her bedroom and sat on the side of her bed. Betsy's father asked about her bad dream, but Betsy couldn't remember much about it.

Her parents thought Betsy might have been upset and had a bad dream because Peter had died. So her mother said, "It is hard to sleep, I know, when someone we have really cared about has died."

"It's not fair!" cried Betsy. "He was just a little boy!"

Her father nodded and said, "Yes, it isn't fair when someone dies who didn't have the chance to grow up and do all the things that grown-ups can do."

Betsy's mother added, "It is very hard to lose a best friend. I know that you will miss Peter very much. Your daddy and I will miss him, too. And do you know what?"

Betsy shook her head and looked up at her mother.

"We also couldn't sleep tonight."

"Because you felt sad, too?" Betsy asked softly.

Her parents nodded, and then they took Betsy in their arms so they all could hold one another.

Betsy was quiet for a bit, and then she started to cry very hard. After a few minutes, her parents asked her what she was thinking. At first Betsy shook her head and said she couldn't tell anyone about it.

"Well," said her mother, "Daddy and I understand if you don't want to talk about it right now. But when you do, we would like very much to hear what you have to say. Because there is *nothing* so terrible that you cannot talk to us about it."

It took a while for Betsy to be able to speak, but then she told her parents that last week she had been angry at Peter. He had spilled paint on her, and Betsy had yelled at him that she *never* wanted to see him again. "But I didn't mean it!" cried Betsy. "I didn't mean it! And now it's come true, and I won't see Peter anymore!"

Betsy's parents told her that everyone gets angry sometimes, and thinks things that may not be nice, but that is *not* the same as doing them. Her father said, "Wishing or thinking things can never make them happen. If that were so, then Peter's parents would be able to wish him back alive, and they cannot do that. It's only in make-believe, like fairy tales and cartoons, that wishing things can make them happen."

"But remember," cried Betsy, "when I wished so hard for a bicycle for my birthday, last year, and then I got it!"

"We remember," said Betsy's mother, "but wishing for your bicycle didn't make it happen. It happened because Daddy and I felt that you were old enough and responsible enough to have a bike of your own."

Betsy felt a little better when her parents told her that. But then she started to think about Peter's parents. "Oh, it's so sad for them. Now they don't have a little boy anymore, to hug them and play with them."

"Yes," said Betsy's mother softly. "It is very sad. I am sure they will miss Peter very much."

"I want to go to Peter's mommy and daddy and give them a big hug and kiss, and maybe that will make them feel better."

"That is a very lovely thought," said her father. "It will be a special comfort to them to be able to talk about Peter with someone who was his good friend. You can share with them the things that Peter said and did, and the things that the two of you did together."

"I know what else I can do," said Betsy. "I can draw them a picture of Peter to keep. And I can also paint a beautiful picture I can hang in *my* room—a special picture to make me remember Peter. Every time I look at it, I will think of him. And when other people look at it, I will tell them that I painted it for Peter, and they will think of him, too."

The next day, Betsy went to school. Peter had been in her class when he was alive. The teacher, Mrs. Brown, asked all the children to sit in a circle so they could talk about Peter and what they remembered most about him.

Sally said that Peter had the reddest hair she had ever seen. The other children agreed. "It was as red as a fire engine," said Billy.

"And he could throw a ball farther than anyone in the class," remembered Joan.

"And when he laughed, he sounded so happy that he made me laugh, too," Sheila added.

"Peter made me mad sometimes," said Jim, "because he didn't like to share."

"Yes," called out Patty. "Sometimes Peter punched me when he got angry."

"But when I fell off my bicycle, Peter held my hand and told me not to cry," remembered Tim.

Mrs. Brown said that, from what everyone was saying, Peter sometimes made children mad, and sometimes he did things to make them feel good. He was his own special person, not exactly like any other boy or girl—just as every boy or girl is special in their own way.

Then Aaron raised his hand and asked, "Is being dead like being asleep? That's what my brother, Joshua, told me."

Mrs. Brown listened carefully and then said, "Sleeping is very different from dying. Sometimes children are confused about the difference, because when we are fast asleep, most of us do not move or speak, and cannot see or hear anything at all. But when people sleep it is only for a short time, to rest their bodies, and they *always* wake up again. When someone dies, it is forever."

The class was quiet for a bit, and then Betsy raised her hand and told the class about the special picture that she was going to paint for Peter. Everyone thought it was a wonderful idea. "Oh, we'd like to paint pictures, too!" said the children. "And we'll put them up on the wall so that everyone who comes into the room will be reminded of Peter."

Mrs. Brown agreed, and said, "When people have lived—even for a short time, like Peter—they stay in the memories of the people who loved them, even after they have died. These memories don't ever go away; they last forever. And that is why Peter will never be forgotten."

51794

J 155.9 C
Cohn, Janice
I had a friend named Peter

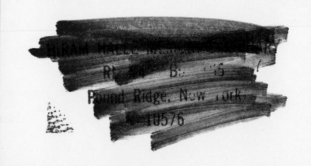